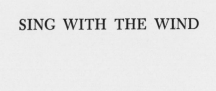

SING WITH THE WIND

Sing
With the
Wind

Words
WINSTON O. ABBOTT

Drawings
BETTE EATON BOSSEN

Published by
INSPIRATION HOUSE
South Windsor, Connecticut

In association with
THE PEQUOT PRESS, INC.
Essex, Connecticut

THIRD PRINTING
1971

This book is a companion volume to
COME WALK AMONG THE STARS
by Winston O. Abbott and
Bette Eaton Bossen

*The author and artist
dedicate these words
and drawings to all
who with searching hearts
have sought the
unseen things*

Because you are a kindred spirit —
                              come —
and stand beside me upon this familiar
hill — where the wind sweeps upward from
the valley — and touches us with its
cooling fragrance —
                    come —
                        and rest for
awhile — and watch the brown grasses gently
nodding — and hear the whispered music of
the oak leaves —
                    here upon this hill — we
are close to the things eternal — you and I —
close to the essential things — the things of
the spirit — the unseen things —
                              here upon
this peaceful hill — the wind sings softly
in the gathering dusk — listen — listen and
let your troubled heart —
                        sing with the wind.

Frail fragile creature

on the cold damp stone —

with restless wings

bright in the April sun —

do you not know

that each must find its own —

that beauty shared

and beauty's need are one —

Faith
    does not come
    in one great flash
as
    lightning of a
    summer night
but
    from a thousand
    tiny lamps
that
    pierce the darkness
    with their light.

There are moments —

        when

        life's theme is played

        upon the muted strings

        but —

        we shall have these

        unforgotten things —

— the flash of color of a bluebird's wings
to match the smiling skies — violets fresh
with dew along the meadow's edge —
fiddleheads beside the brook — the sleepy call
of a robin in the early dawn —
                    black eyed susans and
queen anne's lace — sweet fern fragrant in
the summer sun — indian pipes in the cool
damp woods — green branches holding the sky
above our heads — tree toads talking in the
purple dusk —
                    goldenrod shining with reflected
glory — chickadees calling from the hemlock
branches — the brightly colored sadness of
the autumn hills — falling leaves scratching
little holes in the silence —
                              and —
                                    —
                                    —

— winds that moan among the shivering trees —
snow drifting silently from lowering skies —
stars sparkling like diamonds in the winter
darkness — friendly stars that mark a path
for us across the distant worlds —

                                        and if in
this winter season there should come a night
without stars —

                        we will find our way in the
memory of these — the unforgotten things —

A thousand chosen words
cannot tell the splendor
of a single snowdrop
welcoming the spring —
        nor can
            the greatest artistry of man
            create with purest gold
            the splendor of a single
            autumn leaf —

My wants are few
   but the needs of the spirit are many
   and so —
I have searched with patience
   among the colors of the dawn
   and walked with expectation
   in the sunset's glow —
I have watched the twilight deepen into
   shadow
   and shared the mystery of the night with stars
   I have been a companion of the rain
   and the snow and the fog —
I have felt the peace of a sunlit meadow
   and walked alone into the raging storm
   to listen to the many voices of the wind —
              — and many times —
                 — so many times —

                                    —

                                    —

more times than you will ever know
    I have turned to speak to you
  but you were not there
for you too were searching —
    you also must have known —
  so very long ago
that the needs of the spirit
    are many and great
    and sometimes —
and sometimes unattainable.

Were I to live this life again

I'd still find loneliness and pain —

but what are trivial things like scars

to one who shares the night with stars —

Beauty and love

        these are

               the priceless things —

that feed

     my hungry soul

         and give it wings —

To-night — to-night I saw the naked branches
of the trees reach upward into the flaming
sunset — and amid such indescribable beauty
my heart is touched with the inevitable
sadness — for I know —

that for me — the last
petal must fall from the beautiful rose —
and the last raindrop come to rest upon the
parched earth — and the last haunting note of
the veery echo away into the waiting
darkness —

and I will be alone again — as I
have been alone before —

would it be too much
to ask — that this night be free of clouds —
that I may begin my search anew by the light
of the beckoning stars —

would this be too
much to ask.

There are rare moments —
                    when peace comes
quietly into the waiting heart — if only
for a little while — and the dragonflies
dart here and there above the smiling waters —
and come to rest upon a blade of grass — and
the brook laughs softly as it comes to join
the pond — and the blue heron stands
motionless among the reeds — and the sunlight
soothes the weary body — and the heart is
strangely lifted — if only for a little while —
for the days grow shorter and the nights
grow longer — and —

                    —
                    —

dark blue shadows rest upon the frozen pond —
and the laughter of the brook is stilled —
and the tracks of the hungry deer are marked
upon the newly fallen snow — and the world
is wrapped in the deep silence of winter —
and the yearning heart waits impatiently
and struggles to remember —
                              that in a little
while — the nights will grow shorter again —
and the days will lengthen —
                              and the dragonflies
will come to rest upon a blade of grass.

The mind —

　　　　is bound by many cords
　　　　of logic and of reason
　　　　　　　　while

the heart —

　　　　is often bound by
　　　　the invisible thread
　　　　of a single memory.

The fickle moon looked down upon the shadowed earth — a lone bright lantern hanging in the sky — while in the pond another moon was mirrored in the waters — and I was suspended between the two —

  free from the restraints of earth — while yet a stranger to the sky —

  and
I watched a scudding cloud erase the moon above — and trembled in the darkness until it reappeared — and I saw the ruffled waters shatter the reflection on the surface of the pond — while golden fragments danced upon the ripples — but in another moment the image was restored — as the wind vanished in the night —

  even as faith is sometimes dimmed by life's shadows — and shattered by life's storms — and restored when the winds subside.

The sunlight slants across the rain-washed trees
and comes to rest amid the yellowed ferns —
the raindrops fall in gentle measured beat
a benediction for the heart that yearns —

here in this shadowed woods the darkness waits
until the golden sun has dropped from sight —
while in the twilight burn a million stars
to light our way across the lonely night.

It is not easy to remember

    that in the fading light of day —

        the shadows always point toward

the dawn.

Let
    me
       remember
beyond forgetting —
     let
       me
         remember —

              —
                 —

let me remember always
     for my spirit is often shrouded in the
     mists —
let me remember beyond forgetting
   that my life is not a solitary thing —
     it is a bit of the rushing tide
a leaf of the bending tree —
    a kernel of grain in the golden wheat fields —
     a whisper of wind about the mountaintop —
a reflection of sunlight upon the
       shining waters —
it is fleeting —
         it is of the moment
    it is timeless —
          it is of eternity.

There is something akin to loneliness in the
sound of raindrops falling softly through
the leaves —
        but if you will listen with your
heart — you will hear the carefree laughter
of a brook —
        and beyond that the rushing waters
of a river —
        and beyond that the distant throbbing
of the restless tide —

        —

        — if you will listen
with your heart — you too will know — that a
raindrop is part of the sea — and the sea is
contained in a raindrop —

        —

        — even as love is
a part of eternity — as eternity is born of a
moment of love.

And I remember —
                    standing in the fragrant
orchard and grieving as the pink and white
petals drifted slowly down upon the grass —
                    and this was in the spring —
and I remember —
                    returning after many days had
passed to find the trees bending with the
        burden of the harvest —
                    and it was autumn —
                                                —
                                                —

but life has no seasons —
                    it is a journey from
shadow into the sunlight — and from sunlight
into the shadow again —
                    and from this time of
transition we learn that yesterday and
tomorrow are but the same —
                    and life is real only in the
beauty of this moment —
                    this very moment.

Time does not pass —
  it is motionless
      it is we who pass
  upon its surface —
      as ships
          that sail upon the sea
              from harbor to harbor
      and after a little rest
          embark upon another voyage.

Love

    is a bird of golden wings —

    that —

        flies into your heart

        and sings.

Here — where the ageless hills reach upward
to the ageless stars —here where a century
is measured as a day — I hold these numbered
years called life within my trembling hands —
these fragile years touched with wonder and
with mystery —

there seems to be so little time
in which to learn the purpose for our living —
and yet — in the changeless pattern of things
that are to be — there must be both meaning
and purpose — or we would be insensitive to the
healing power of beauty — and the sustaining
power of love —

perhaps I am here to touch but a
single heart — or to fill a single need — or to
share my strength with one who needs a shield
against a hostile world —

I do not know — perhaps
it is destined that I should not know — but
another may know —

and understand —

and be grateful.

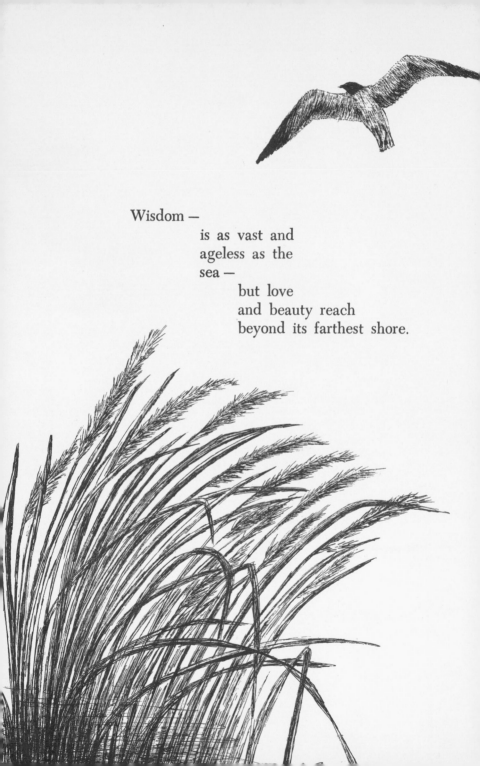

Wisdom —

      is as vast and
      ageless as the
      sea —
            but love
            and beauty reach
            beyond its farthest shore.

Come share with me —
                    the mystery of this
                    brightly jewelled night —
for —
    once you have heard the singing of
    the stars —
                    you are no longer a
                    prisoner of the earth.

It was because I did not know —
that I asked
        what is beauty —
                and then
I saw a toad sitting beneath a garden lily
              and I wondered
if the toad was admiring the lily —
or the lily the toad —
        and —
           this is how
I came to understand
that beauty is of the spirit
we cannot hold it in our mortal hands
only in the cloister of our hearts
and this we must always remember —
        both you and I
for the world sometimes forgets.

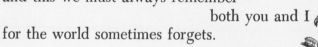

Life is filled with many seeming contradictions
for —
joy that is shared
grows even greater
while
sadness shared
is lessened.

Perhaps

     it was by chance

but

    I cannot be sure

there is so much of mystery

    in the simplest things —

so much of grandeur

    in the commonplace

       and —

           —

           —

it did come to rest
    upon my outstretched hand
a single milkweed seed
a tiny brown speck
    an infinitesimal bit of life
drifting across the meadow —
was it by chance too
    that in that very moment
I could see beyond
        my life's horizon
        for —
            I had held
            the future
                in my hand.

We need so very much to know — both you
and I
        that raindrops
            lying colorless upon the grass
        reflect
            the rainbow
            in the lighted heart.

How tiny are the lamps of fireflies moving
in the scented dusk — how feeble are their
lights where lightning marks the brooding
storm — and fills the starless sky with
yellow flame — how feeble are their lights —
and yet they go their way above the ripening
grasses unafraid and free —
                              until the
drenching rains put out their lamps and thunder
shakes the earth where they have taken refuge
from the storm —
                   but —
                           soon the rains will go
to other meadows — and the grasses will
struggle to free themselves from the sodden
earth — and the tiny lamps will be lighted once
again and move undaunted through the drip-
ping darkness — can a tiny insect know that
this night will have no other light until the stars
return.

The world is strangely stilled —
                              but there
should be no sorrow — as another day ebbs
away upon the endless tide of time —
                              and the
crimson turns to ashes — and the gold is
tarnished — and the pale greens lose their
luster — and the mauve that follows in their
wake is lost in the graying sky —
                              and —
                                    the
shadows fall behind us — and unbidden tears
glisten in the fading light —
                              for you once
told me long ago — that the night has not the
power to hide such glory — and if we turn our
backs upon the fading splendor — we shall find
even greater promise — in the flush of
to-morrow's dawn.

Where I have searched — I have always found
an answer — as once I found a single yellow
blossom — not in the sunlit fields — but in
the deeply shaded woods — a single unfamiliar
yellow flower — perhaps destined never to be
seen by other eyes — five rounded golden
petals — with shiny oval leaves upon a slender
stalk —

     I reached down to claim it as my own
but some strange force restrained me —
something that I could not understand —

                         —

                      —

                        —

was this solitary flower seeded by some bird
in flight — or was there another purpose
for its existence in this sheltered and
secluded place —
           that afternoon I did not
know — but days have come and gone and now
I do — and because I left it blossoming where
it had struggled upward from the forest floor —
I can claim its beauty for my own —
                         for it has
become a part of me — for I have searched and
I have found my answer.

Nature

      through the endless cycle of the seasons

      tirelessly

           strives for perfection —

and who are we

           but nature's children.

Here in this silver cocoon — here within
this sheltering leaf — life lies quietly
sleeping — motionless against the time of
its awakening —
            and I wonder —
            will the emerging moth know
that it was once a creature of lesser beauty —
            and yet — I should not wonder
for I cannot recall the life before my birth —
even though there are rare moments of
awareness — and I am certain that yesterday is
not entirely forgotten —
            some tiny spark burns through the
enfolding darkness — and I am at the very edge
of remembering — but only for a moment —
                                    for an
even greater wisdom decrees that a spark shall
glow only for the instant —
            and is extinguished
in the night.

Light is not lost
            when this bright day is gone
there comes a time of dark
            and then the dawn —
man does not die
            when spirit leaves the earth
he has but gone to know
            another birth.

There is strength in gentleness
  and there is gentleness in strength
  but this I did not always know
until one day I saw
  a single strand of spider web hold fast
            against the fury of the storm
  and watched
on a remembered April afternoon
  as the Mourning Cloak fluttered on feeble
  wings to shake off the numbness of the
                              winter's cold
and in this struggle found greater reverence
  for the gentle creatures of the earth
  and in the fragile wings of a butterfly
found renewed strength for my spirit
                              and came
      to better understand
there is a strength in gentleness.

So many times —
             mere words
             fall useless
                        to the ground —
             and
only then in the silence
                   can
                   the truth
                        be heard.

The storm is spent —
                    and in the brooding
dusk — small wisps of fog appear — to
wander aimlessly above the rain-washed
earth —
          even as memories rise in the misty
twilight — to ease the loneliness — that
deepens as the darkness comes.

We walk but a little way together — so may
our footsteps linger —
                        and may there be
flowers along our path — that we may hold the
fragrant blossoms in our hands —
                        remembering
that they came to grow in the fields without
assistance from you or from me — they were
planted in some mysterious way — and having
added color to the meadow — bowed their
heads and died —
            but death is brief — for there
will come another spring — and fresh new
    beauty for the waiting earth —
                        may we walk a little
farther — until we really know — that beauty
like love — is but another name for immortality.

Slowly
    ever so slowly
        you and I shall come to know
        and perhaps to understand
        that
        the strength
      that throbs
    within these restless wings
      is such
        as we have found
          in unseen
            things.

PUBLISHER'S NOTE

It is rare indeed when an author and artist work together with such complete accord to portray and interpret the intangible beauty of life. If you have enjoyed this book you will also appreciate the companion volume, COME WALK AMONG THE STARS, with drawings by Bette Eaton Bossen and words by Winston O. Abbott. This is another publication of

INSPIRATION HOUSE
SOUTH WINDSOR
CONNECTICUT